My Best Book of
Ponies

Jackie Budd

KINGFISHER

Contents

Author: Jackie Budd
Consultant: Lesley Ward
Senior editor: Sarah Milan
Editor: Camilla Reid
Senior designer: Sarah Goodwin
Designer: Ruth Levy
Cover design: Mike Davis
Production controller: Kelly Johnson
Illustrators: Lindsay Graham,
Kaye Hodges, Christian Hook

KINGFISHER
Kingfisher Publications Plc,
New Penderel House,
283–288 High Holborn,
London WC1V 7HZ

First published by Kingfisher
Publications Plc 1999

(hb) 10 9 8 7 6 5 4 3 2
2TR/0499/WKT/MAR(MAR)/128KMA
(pb) 10 9 8 7 6 5 4 3 2 1
(1SCA)/0499/WKT/MAR(MAR)/128KMA

Copyright © Kingfisher
Publications Plc 1999

A CIP catalogue record for this book
is available from the British Library.

ISBN 0 7534 0303 X (hb)
      0 7534 0425 7 (pb)

Printed in Hong Kong / China

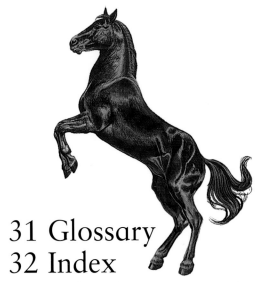

A foal is born

In a grassy paddock on a summer's day, a foal nestles close to his mother. Although it is only a few hours since he was born, he is up on his long, wobbly legs. His ears flick to and fro, curious about the other ponies in the field and the world around him. In a day or two, he may feel brave enough to meet the rest of the foals and join in the game they are playing. For now, he feels safe by the mare's side.

Making friends

A little foal has lots to discover. He must learn all about life with other ponies. And by being handled every day, he will get used to being around people too. When he is about four years old, he can be trained to take a rider on his back.

All about ponies

There are so many fascinating facts to learn about ponies. Perhaps you have met ponies at a riding school, or you may even have a pony of your own. Discover all you can about them and you will soon become the best of friends.

Colours and markings

Ponies come in all kinds of colours, each with its own name. To tell the difference between them, look out for the colour of the coat, and of the mane and tail.

Often there are white markings on the face and legs – these have special names too. Learn these terms so that you can easily describe a particular pony.

How many hands?

A pony is a small horse. All horses are measured in 'hands', which are units of 4 inches (10 centimetres). Ponies measure 14 hands and 2 inches or less.

Stripe

Snip

Sock

Bay Brown coat with a black mane and tail

Black Black coat and a black mane and tail

Blaze

Stocking

Chestnut Red-brown colour all over

Palomino Golden coat with a pale mane and tail

The points of a pony

The parts of a pony are called 'points'. They each have a different name.

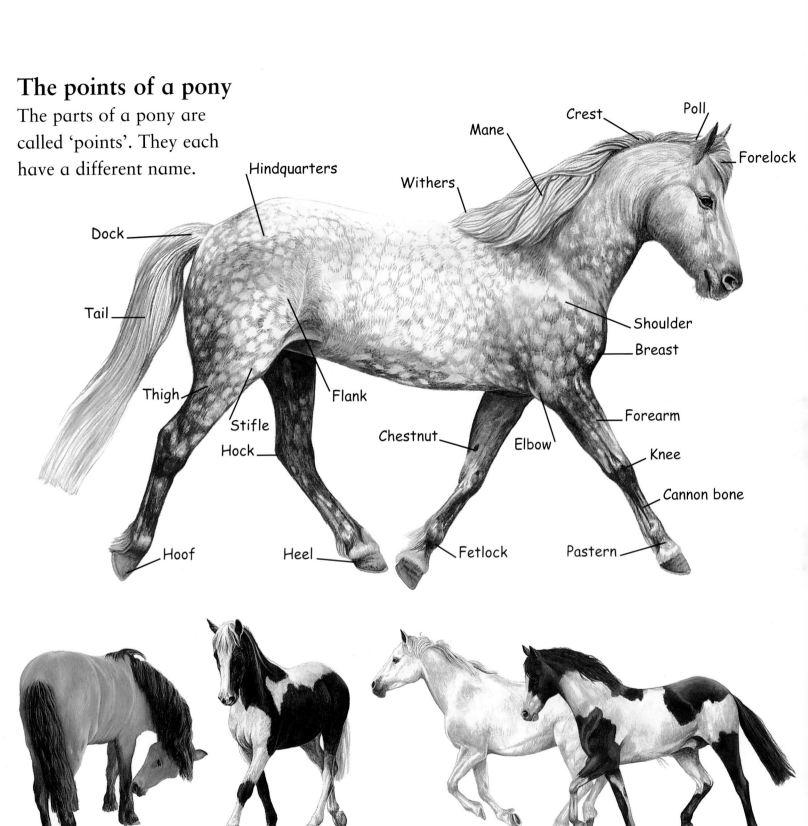

Hindquarters

Mane

Crest

Poll

Forelock

Withers

Dock

Shoulder

Breast

Tail

Forearm

Thigh

Flank

Chestnut

Elbow

Knee

Stifle

Hock

Cannon bone

Hoof

Heel

Fetlock

Pastern

Dun Pale brown coat with a black mane and tail

Piebald Large patches of black and white

Grey White or grey coat. A dark grey coat with light grey rings is called dapple grey

Skewbald Large patches of brown and white

7

Horses and ponies of the world

Horses and ponies are found all over the world. In each region, breeds have developed to suit the conditions there. And for thousands of years, humans have used these strong, speedy animals to help them in their lives.

Sable Island pony
USA

Mustang
USA

Morgan
USA

Appaloosa
USA

Quarter horse
USA

Criollo
Argentina

Falabella miniature horse
Argentina

On the ranch

One of the horse's earliest jobs was to help a rider keep up with a herd on the move. In North and South America, fast and agile horses are still used to help round up cattle.

Fun and games

The invention of machines has meant there are fewer working horses and ponies to be found today. Now we enjoy training them for sports and other activities. These riders are playing a game of polo.

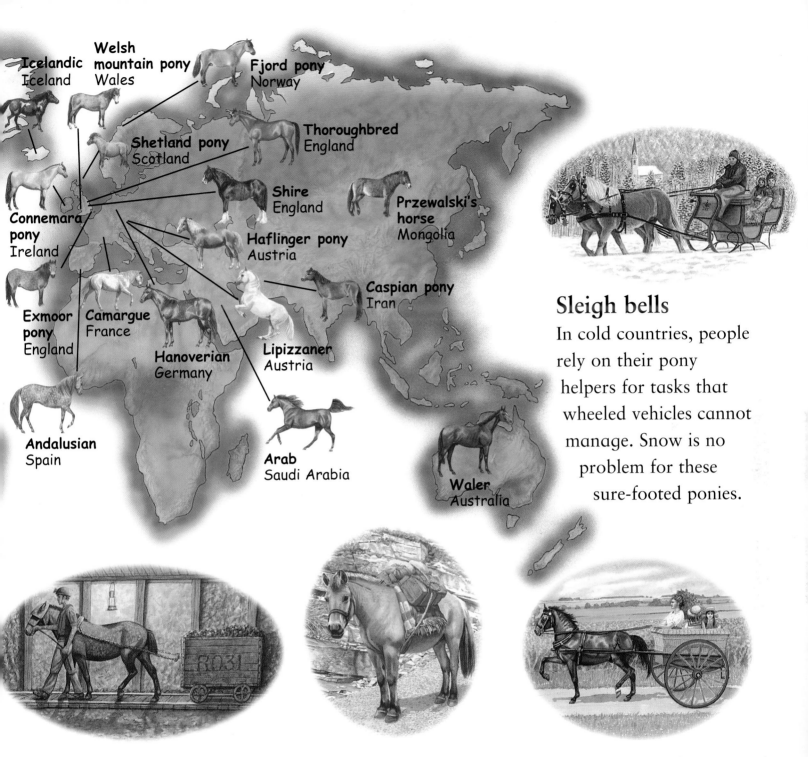

Icelandic
Iceland

Welsh
mountain pony
Wales

Fjord pony
Norway

Shetland pony
Scotland

Thoroughbred
England

Shire
England

Przewalski's
horse
Mongolia

Connemara
pony
Ireland

Haflinger pony
Austria

Caspian pony
Iran

Exmoor
pony
England

Camargue
France

Lipizzaner
Austria

Hanoverian
Germany

Andalusian
Spain

Arab
Saudi Arabia

Waler
Australia

Sleigh bells

In cold countries, people rely on their pony helpers for tasks that wheeled vehicles cannot manage. Snow is no problem for these sure-footed ponies.

Pit ponies

Ponies were pulling carts deep down inside coal mines until recent years. It must have been a dark and dirty job, and very hard work.

Packing up

In many mountainous countries, ponies are used to carry heavy loads. Survival here would be hard without these sturdy workers.

Getting around

Throughout history, ponies have been harnessed to carts and carriages to transport people and goods over long distances.

9

Ponies of the past

Ponies like these lived over 12,000 years ago. They survived because they had sharp eyes for spotting hunters – like this sabre-toothed tiger – and fast legs for carrying them away from danger. No wonder modern ponies are such wary creatures, always on the alert for the slightest noise or movement.

Life in a herd

Ponies love company and, by sticking together in a herd, they feel safe. In any group of ponies some will always become special friends.

Just like humans, every pony will have its own personality too. Some may have bossy or grumpy characters, some will be brave and friendly, others timid and shy.

Handle with care

The natural instincts of their ancestors still exist in ponies today. They are friendly animals but, even when trained, they can be startled easily. Because of this, it is important to take care around ponies. Learning about them will give you confidence and help you to win their trust.

Contented

Curious

Angry

Interested

On the look-out

Stay alert when you are riding. Your pony may see or hear something that surprises him and, as a wild pony would do, he may take fright.

Making faces

Ponies may feel excited, happy or angry, just like we do. Sometimes you can tell what a pony is thinking or feeling by the look on his face and the way he holds his body.

Catching a pony

1 Whenever you are with ponies try to be relaxed and calm. If you have to catch a pony in a field, walk towards him slowly so that he can see you approaching. Hold the headcollar down by your side and speak quietly to him.

2 The headcollar and lead-rope are used to lead and tie up a pony. First place the lead-rope around the pony's neck then reward him with a titbit.

3 Avoiding any sudden movements, put the pony's nose through the headcollar. Lift the strap behind his ears and buckle it up. Praise him and stroke him firmly on the neck.

4 Walk alongside the pony's head, holding the lead-rope underneath the chin. Hold the rest of the lead-rope in your other hand.

13

The outdoor pony

Ponies enjoy the outdoor life, as this is what they would be used to in the wild. In a field, ponies can roam freely with their friends and eat grass, which is their natural food. The field must have strong fencing, fresh water and shelter. A pony living outside must be visited twice a day to check that he is all right.

A coat for all seasons

In winter, ponies grow a thick coat to protect them from the cold, though ponies with finer fur may need a waterproof rug to help keep them warm. All year round, there is nothing a pony likes more than a roll – it feels good and helps to keep the coat healthy.

Stable mates

Some ponies live in stables all year round, others may spend only a few hours a day indoors. A pony's stable must be large and airy so that he is free to move and lie down. The stable yard should have secure, rat-proof rooms in which to keep feed and tack. Tools and equipment must be stored neatly to prevent accidents.

Safety first
It is very important that no one smokes in the stable yard.

The tack room
Tack is the gear a pony wears for riding, and it is kept in the tack room. Tack must be cleaned after every ride so it is kept supple and safe to use.

Bedding down
The pony's bed should keep the pony warm at night and be comfortable when he is lying down. There are several types of bedding to choose from.

Wood shavings

Shredded paper

Straw

Feed facts

When a pony is in the stable, he will need hay (dried grass) to eat. If he is being ridden, he may also need one of these other feeds to keep him healthy and energetic.

Pony nuts

Coarse mix

Apples and carrots

Haynet

17

Daily tasks

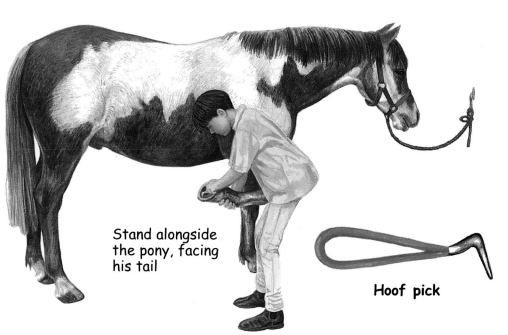

Each day, all year long, there are jobs to do to keep a pony happy and healthy. He needs food and water, and both he and his home must be kept clean and tidy. Caring for a pony can be hard work, but it can also be good fun.

Smart and shiny

Grooming keeps the coat glossy and the skin clean. Make sure the pony is tied up, then remove any surface dirt with the dandy brush before working over the coat with the body brush.

Stand alongside the pony, facing his tail

Hoof pick

Feet first

The hooves should be picked out twice a day. Run your hand down the leg then ask him to lift his foot by giving the fetlock a tug. Working from heel to toe, remove any mud or bedding.

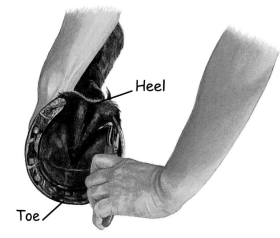

Heel

Toe

Dandy brush removes dried mud and sweat

Rubber curry comb for very muddy or hairy ponies

Body brush for cleaning the coat

Sponge gives the eyes, nose and dock a refreshing wash

Sweatscraper wipes off extra water after a bath

The grooming kit

Grooming a pony is a great way to get to know him. Even if you don't own a pony, you can collect all the brushes and tools you'll need to look after your favourite riding school pony.

Mucking out

Stables must be mucked out every day. Lift out the droppings and wet patches with a fork, and put them into a wheelbarrow. Finally, put in the new, dry bedding.

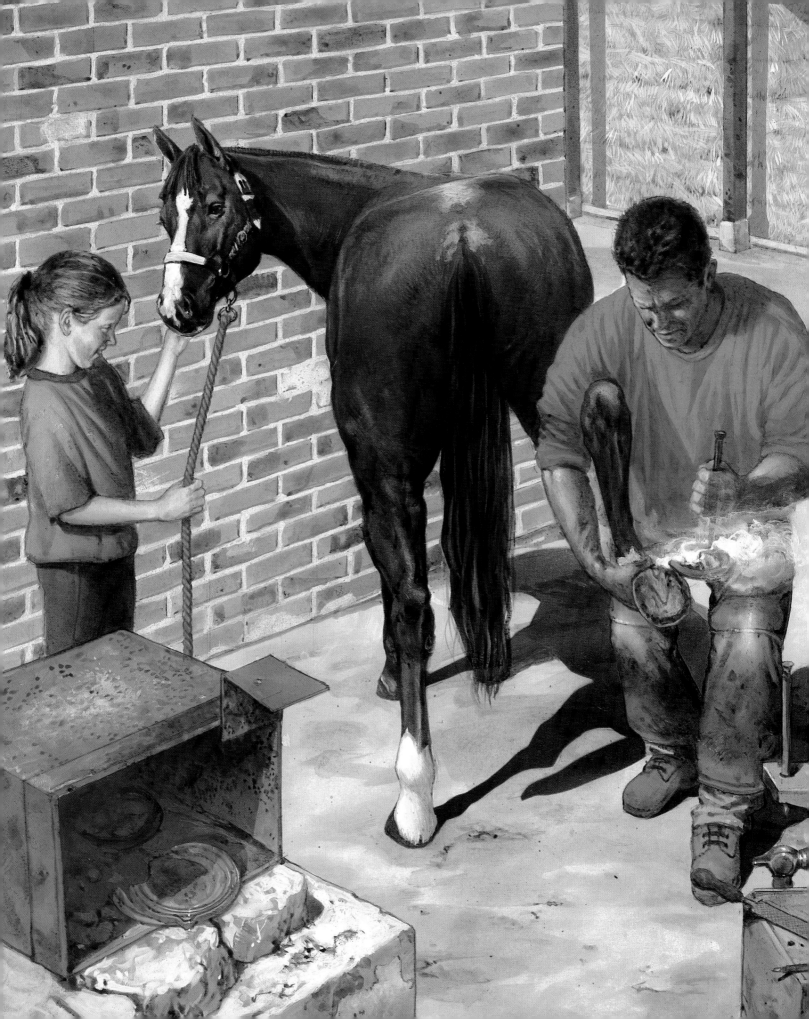

Feeling fit

Bright eyes, a shiny coat and a lively expression show that a pony is feeling fit and healthy.

To keep him this way, a pony should be well cared for. His feet must be checked regularly by a farrier. If ever he is ill or injured, the vet must be called out to treat him.

New shoes

Without metal horseshoes, a pony who is ridden would soon get sore feet. Every few weeks, the farrier must visit to take off old shoes, trim the pony's hooves and fit a new set of shoes. Just like our fingernails, hooves grow all the time, so even ponies that don't wear shoes must have their feet trimmed.

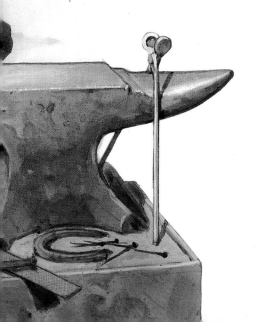

The vet's visit

The vet will look after a pony in an emergency, but vets also help with the routine healthcare that all ponies need. She may check that the teeth are in good condition. She will also vaccinate the pony against disease and give him medicine to stop him getting parasites known as 'worms'.

Bridles and bits

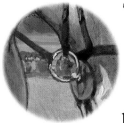

The bridle is used to control the pony when he is being ridden. It is important that the bridle fits properly and is kept clean, so the pony is comfortable and happy.

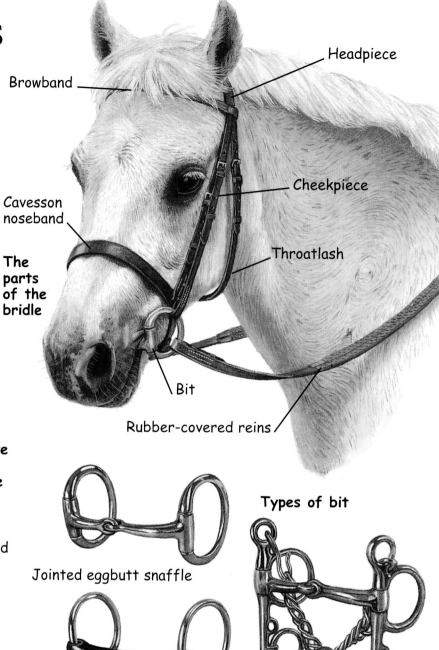

Browband

Headpiece

Cheekpiece

Cavesson noseband

The parts of the bridle

Throatlash

Bit

Rubber-covered reins

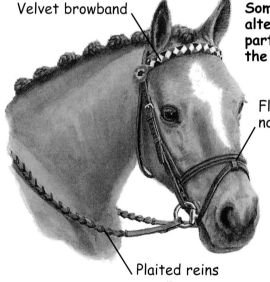

Velvet browband

Some alternative parts of the bridle

Flash noseband

Plaited reins

Jointed eggbutt snaffle

Types of bit

Straight-bar rubber snaffle

Jointed Pelham

What is a bridle?
The bridle is a set of leather straps. The different parts can be changed to suit you and your pony's needs.

Choosing a bit
The bit lies over the pony's tongue and is connected to the reins and cheekpieces. There are many bits to choose from. Most ponies wear a snaffle, which has a ring at each side and can be jointed or straight. Livelier ponies may need a Pelham.

How to put on a bridle

1 Take the reins over the pony's head. Hold the bridle in your right hand and slip the bit into the mouth with your left hand.

2 Raise the headpiece over the ears, then pull the forelock from under the browband. Check that the bit just wrinkles the mouth.

3 When fastened, you should be able to fit four fingers between the throatlash and the cheek. Finally, buckle the noseband.

Western riding

In the United States and some other parts of the world, Western riding is very popular. For this style of riding, the pony wears a different set of tack. Western bridles have no noseband and are often beautifully decorated. Only a very light touch on the reins is needed.

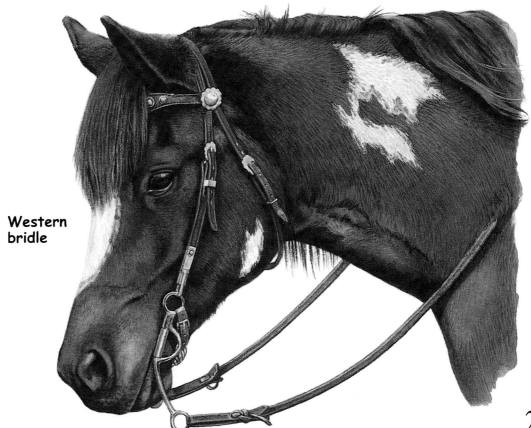

Western bridle

23

Saddling up

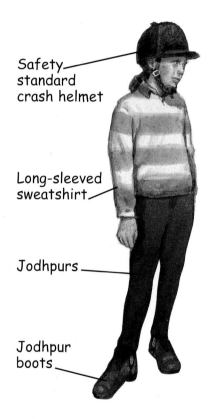

A saddle helps the rider sit securely in the best position on the pony's back. In this picture, the boy is using a Western saddle and the girl an English one. The saddle is fastened around the pony's tummy by a thick strap called the girth.

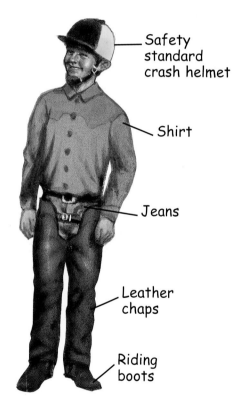

Safety standard crash helmet

Long-sleeved sweatshirt

Jodhpurs

Jodhpur boots

Safety standard crash helmet

Shirt

Jeans

Leather chaps

Riding boots

English style
English-style riding clothes are designed to be smart and safe. Most important are boots with a heel and a good hat.

Western style
Western-style riding gear is based on the clothes used by cowboys on the ranch. It is comfortable and very hard-wearing.

Learning to ride

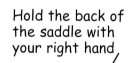

The best place to learn to ride is at a riding school where instructors can make the lessons safe and fun.

Your instructor will help you choose a pony that is right for you and teach you how to tell the pony what you want him to do.

Stirrup iron   Stirrup leather

Stirrup leathers

Check that the stirrup leathers are the correct length by putting your fist on the buckle and the stirrup iron under your arm.

Mounting

Stand on the left side of the pony, facing the tail, with the reins in your left hand. Put your left foot in the stirrup. Hold the back of the saddle and swing your leg over the pony's hindquarters.

Hold the back of the saddle with your right hand

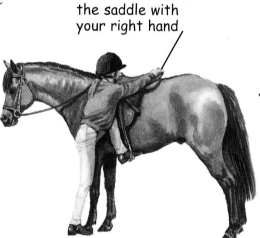

Swing your leg clear of the pony's back

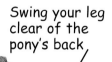

Dismounting

To get off a pony safely, first take both feet out of the stirrups. Lean forwards, swing your right leg over the pony's back, and jump to the ground.

Getting started

It is important to sit well in the saddle. To ask the pony to go faster, to slow down, or to turn, you will use signals called the 'aids'. These are given using your legs, hands, voice and seat (your bottom!).

Look straight ahead

Relax but sit up straight

Keep your elbows bent

Rest the ball of your foot on the stirrup, with your heels down

Hold the reins with your thumbs on top and little fingers underneath

Trot on

A pony has four paces – walk, trot, canter and gallop. Trotting is very bumpy until you learn to rise to the trot. This means you have to rise up and sit down with his steps.

The canter

As your riding improves, you can try a canter. Ask the pony to speed up by nudging your heels inwards. Sit down and enjoy the ride!

Going to a show

'And it's a clear round!' There is nothing more exciting than winning a rosette on your favourite pony. When you get better at riding, you can learn to jump and even have the chance to enter a show. Jumping needs plenty of practice. Remember to look up, sit quietly in the saddle and keep in balance over the fence. You and your pony have to be a real team.

Ready, steady, go!
These riders are taking part in a sack race at a show. Gymkhana events, or mounted games, are like party games on horseback. From the egg and spoon race to the bending race, all the games are fast, furious – and great fun. To be a winner, you'll need both skill and speed.

Pony fun

There is no end to the thrills and challenges of riding a pony. Whichever type of riding you choose, there is a whole world of fun waiting for you.

Out and about

Exploring the countryside on board a pony with a group of friends is always exciting. Together you can ride through woods, across fields – or even head for the hills.

Vaulting

Acrobatics on horseback is called vaulting. Having a go at vaulting will help your riding skills, as it teaches you to stay perfectly balanced.

Forever friends

Perhaps you would like to have your own pony, or become a famous rider one day. Maybe you just want to spend time with a four-legged friend. Whatever your pony dream, have fun!

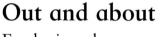

Glossary

aid A signal used by the rider to tell the pony what to do. There are four aids a rider can use – the hands, legs, seat and voice. Another aid that may be useful is a whip.

bridle The headgear that the pony wears for riding.

clear round When you complete a jumping course without making any mistakes, you have done a clear round.

colt A male pony under four years old.

cross-country An event which takes place in the countryside, where pony and rider attempt a course of natural jumps.

farrier A person trained to fit ponies' shoes.

filly A female pony under four years old.

foal A baby pony.

gelding A male pony who cannot father foals.

graze To eat fresh grass.

groom To brush a pony.

gymkhana games Mounted games, or races on horseback.

hand The unit of measurement used to describe a pony's height. It is so called because this is about the width of an adult's hand. One hand is four inches (10 centimetres) wide. Horses are 14 hands and 3 inches, or above, in height. Ponies measure 14 hands and 2 inches, or under.

hay Cut, dried grass.

headcollar A piece of tack used on the pony's head for catching, leading and tying up.

mare An adult female pony.

mount To get on a pony. Getting off a pony is called dismounting.

near side The left side of the pony (from his point of view).

off side The right side of the pony (from his point of view).

points The parts of the pony.

saddle The item of equipment used on the pony's back to keep the rider in position. It is usually made of leather and is held in place by the girth, which fastens round the pony's tummy. The stirrup leathers and stirrup irons attach to the saddle and support the rider's feet.

show An event where ponies and riders can compete in either showing classes, jumping classes or gymkhana events.

show jumping A jumping class at a show that takes place in an arena, over brightly coloured fences.

stallion An adult male pony used for breeding.

tack All the gear needed to ride a pony, which includes the saddle and bridle.

Index